Doodles Help Pre Handwriting: Shapes and Dino Fun

Sarah Muldoon, OTR/L

About This Book

Learning about shapes is a foundation for handwriting, math and beyond. Recognizing and drawing shapes develops visual discrimination, spatial awareness, problem solving, and fine motor skills. This further opens up language development which makes geometry, math, and engineering concepts more accessible. Ideas like a triangle or square having "sides" and "corners" changes the way children look at the world. Now, how to make it fun for little learners? You guessed it, DINOSAURS!

I created Doodles Help Pre Handwriting: Shapes and Dino Fun to make learning shapes gigantically fun and exciting. Research shows that exposure to early experiences with shapes and patterns significantly predicts later writing abilities! Children as young as 3 can start to imitate simple lines and shapes. If you are helping a child with this book and the doodling activities are above their skill level, you can have them trace and color the steps, make dots to connect the lines, or have them watch you make the doodles. Sticky notes, squares of paper and the blank pages in this book make great extra drawing spaces.

If you are one of the special people working with young children and want to share your experiences or doodles please email me at sarahmuldoon@doodleshelphandwriting.com, or find me on Instagram @doodles_help_handwriting. I am always willing to answer any questions or hear any feedback to make Doodles Help Handwriting better, so don't hesitate to ask! Thank you for buying this book. Happy tiny doodling!

Trace the Circle

A circle is tall as it is wide!

How many circles make up the Dino Eyes?

Good answer! Now turn the page to doodle Dino Eyes!

Extra Drawing Space!

Dino Eyes

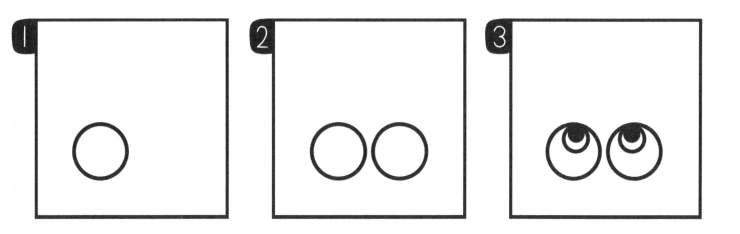

Extra Drawing Space!

Trace the Oval

An oval is like a circle that has been squashed! It is longer than it is wide, or wider than it is long!

Is the Dino Egg an oval?

Good answer! Now turn the page to doodle a Dino Egg!

Extra Drawing Space!

Dino Egg

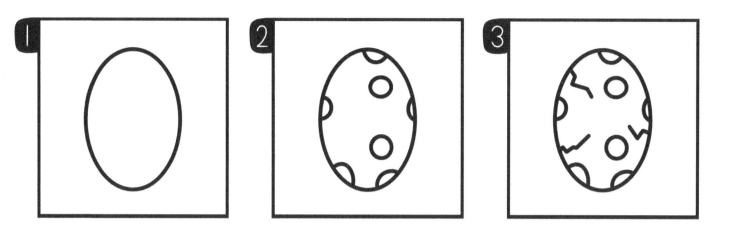

Extra Drawing Space!

Trace the Egg and color the picture.

Trace the Oval

An oval is an oval if it is sitting up or on its side!

What part of the Plesiosaurus is an oval?

Good answer! Now turn the page to doodle a Plesiosaurus!

Extra Drawing Space!

Plesiosaurus

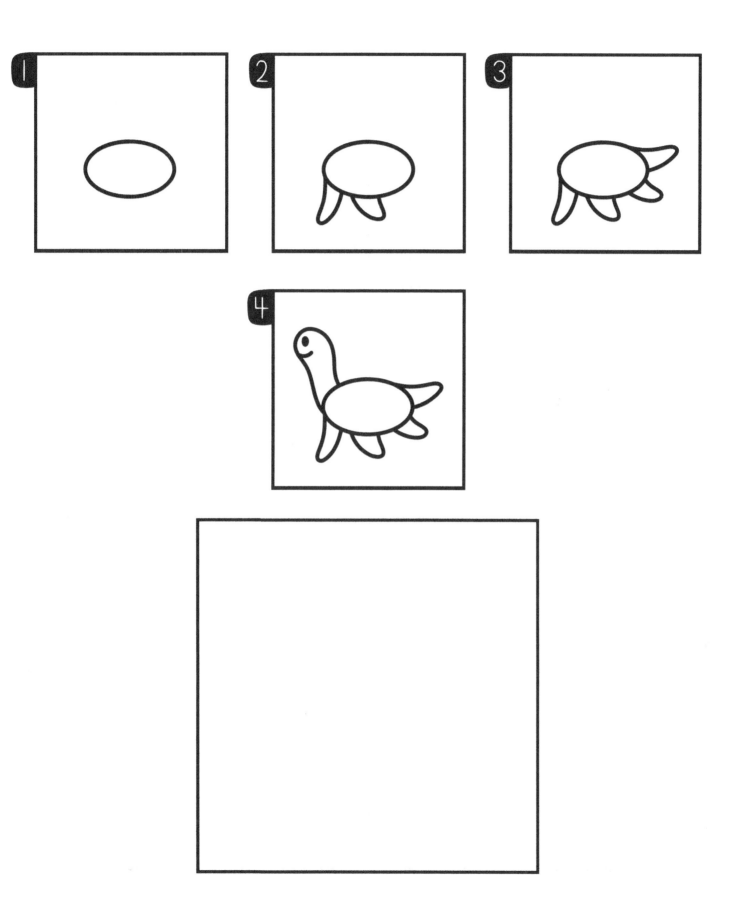

Extra Drawing Space!

Trace the Plesiosaurus and color the picture.

Trace the Oval

An oval
has no
corners!

How is the Palm Leaf doodle like
an oval? How is it different?

Good answer!
Now turn the page to
doodle a palm leaf!

Extra Drawing Space!

Palm Leaf

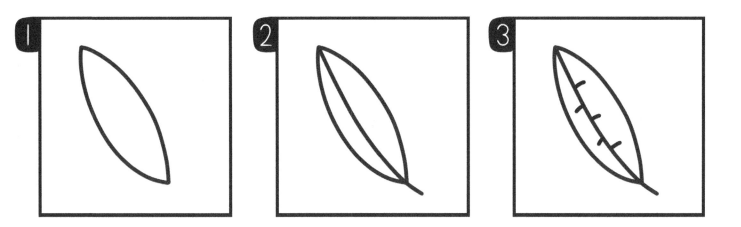

Extra Drawing Space!

Trace the Palm Leaf and color the picture.

Trace the Semi Circle

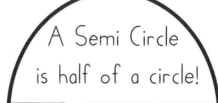

A Semi Circle is half of a circle!

How many Semi Circles are in the Archeologist Hat doodle?

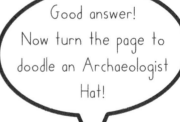

Good answer! Now turn the page to doodle an Archaeologist Hat!

Extra Drawing Space!

Archeologist Hat

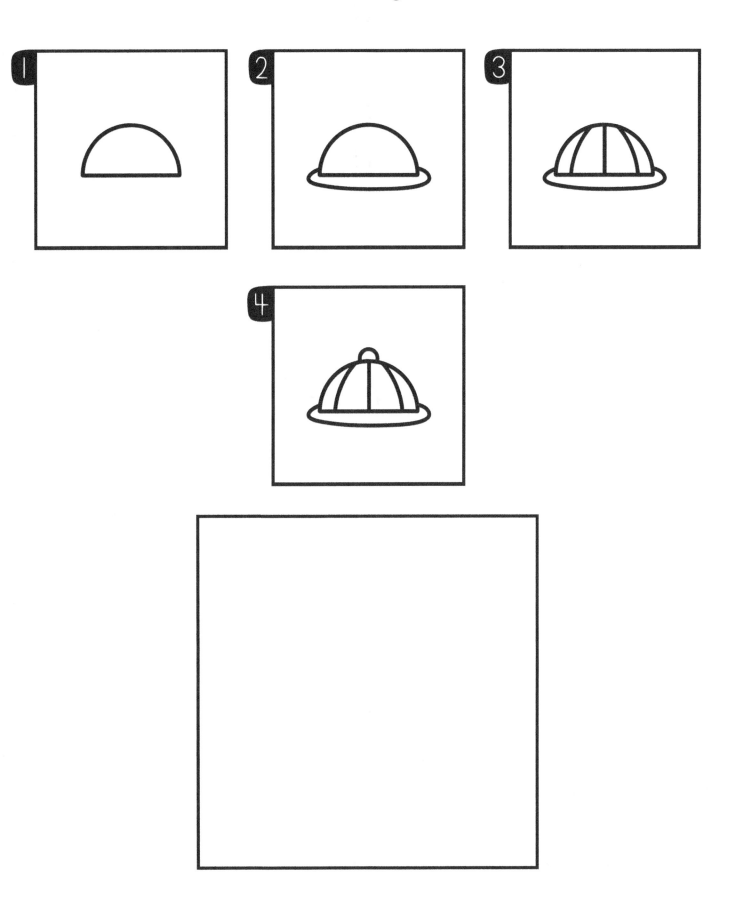

Extra Drawing Space!

Trace the Archeologist
Hat and color the picture.

Trace the Semi Circle

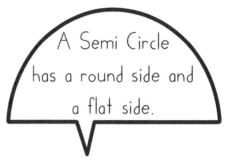

A Semi Circle has a round side and a flat side.

What part of the Stegosaurus doodle is a semi circle?

Good answer! Now turn the page to doodle a Stegosaurus!

Extra Drawing Space!

Stegosaurus

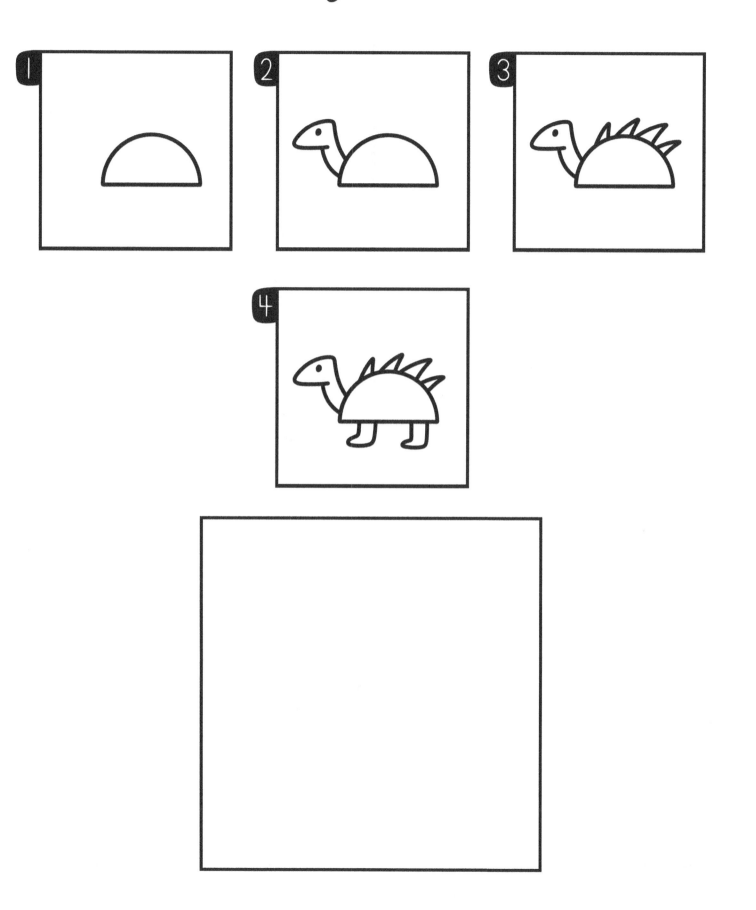

Extra Drawing Space!

Trace the Stegosaurus and color the picture.

Trace the Triangle

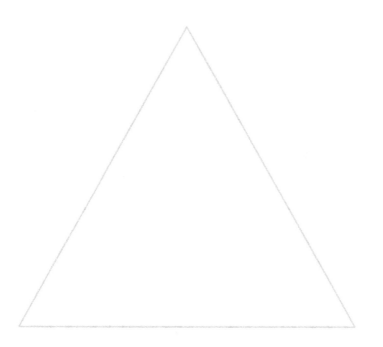

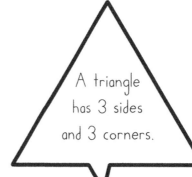
A triangle has 3 sides and 3 corners.

What part of the Dino Poop is a triangle?

Good answer! Now turn the page to doodle a dino poop!

Extra Drawing Space!

Dino Poop

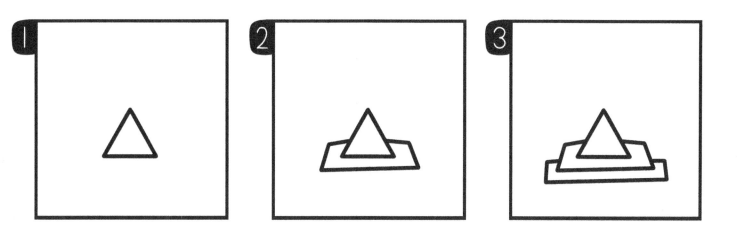

Extra Drawing Space!

Trace the Dino Poop and color the picture.

Trace the Triangle

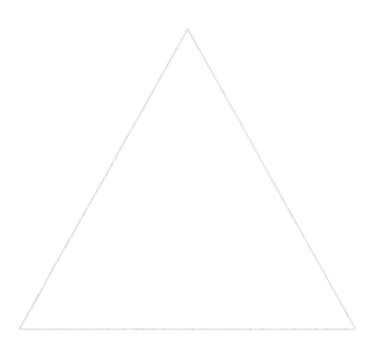

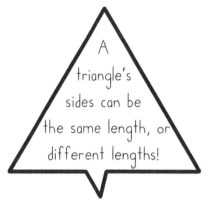

A triangle's sides can be the same length, or different lengths!

How is the Volcano doodle like a triangle? How is it different?

Good answer! Now turn the page to doodle a volcano!

Extra Drawing Space!

Volcano

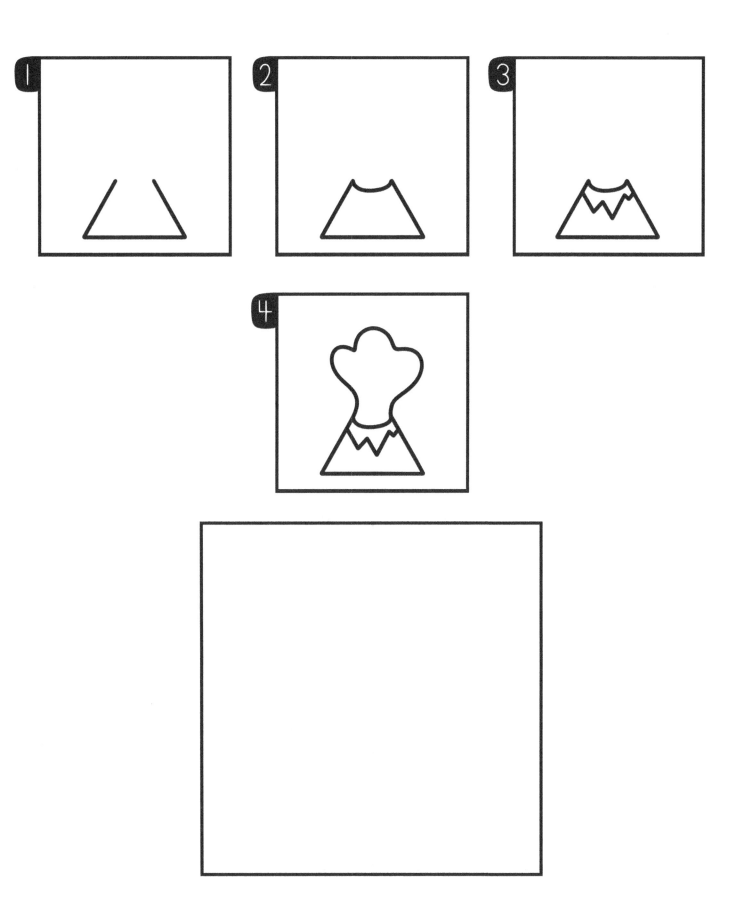

Extra Drawing Space!

Trace the Volcano and color the picture.

Trace the Triangle

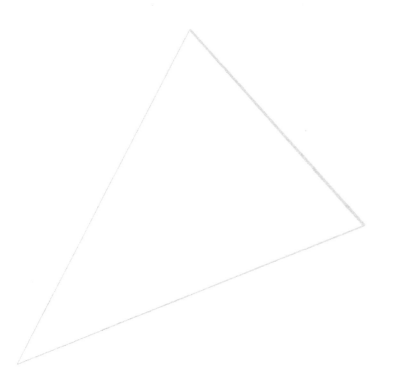

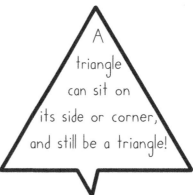

A triangle can sit on its side or corner, and still be a triangle!

What part of the Pterodactyl Head has 3 sides and 3 corners?

Good answer! Now turn the page to doodle a pterodactyl head!

Extra Drawing Space!

Pterodactyl Head

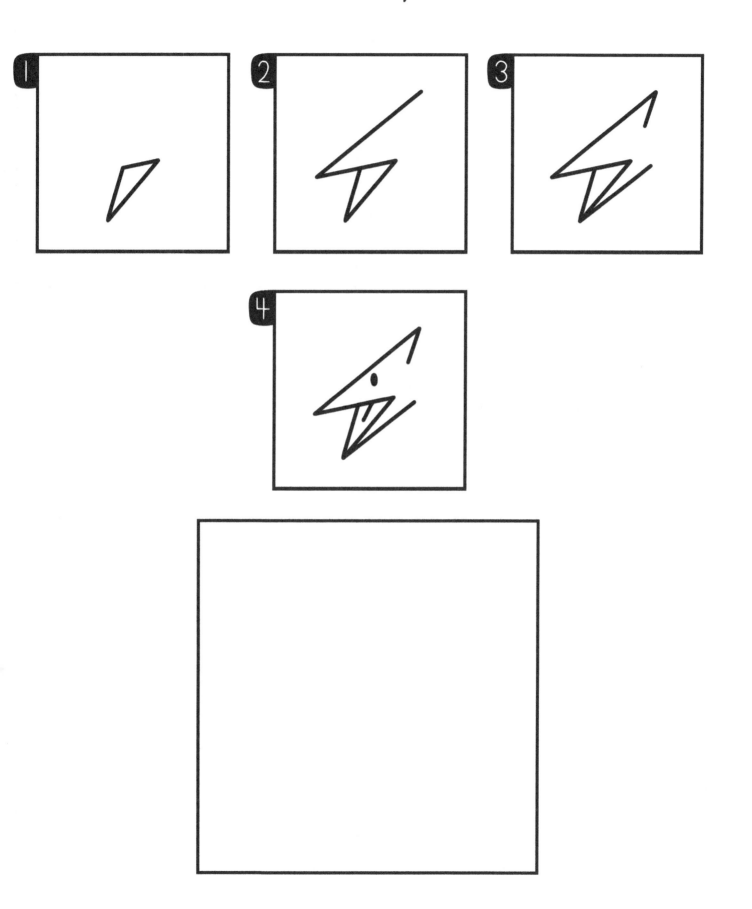

Extra Drawing Space!

Trace the Pterodactyl Head and color the picture.

Trace the Square

A square has 4 sides that are all the same length, and 4 corners too!

Can you trace the square in the Toast doodle with your finger?

Good job! Now turn the page to doodle Dino Toast!

Extra Drawing Space!

Dino Toast

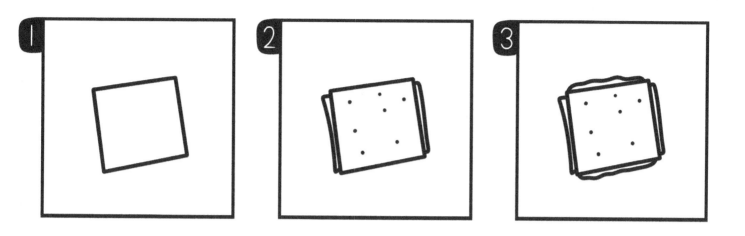

Extra Drawing Space!

Trace the Toast and color the picture.

Trace the Rectangle

A rectangle is like a square, but has two long sides and two shorter sides.

What part of the Toothbrush doodle is a rectangle?

Good answer! Now turn the page to doodle a Dino Toothbrush!

Extra Drawing Space!

Dino Toothbrush

Extra Drawing Space!

Trace the Toothbrush and color the picture.

Trace the Rectangle

A rectangle can be short or long!

How many rectangles can you count in the fossil brush?

Good answer! Now turn the page to doodle a Fossil Brush!

Extra Drawing Space!

Fossil Brush

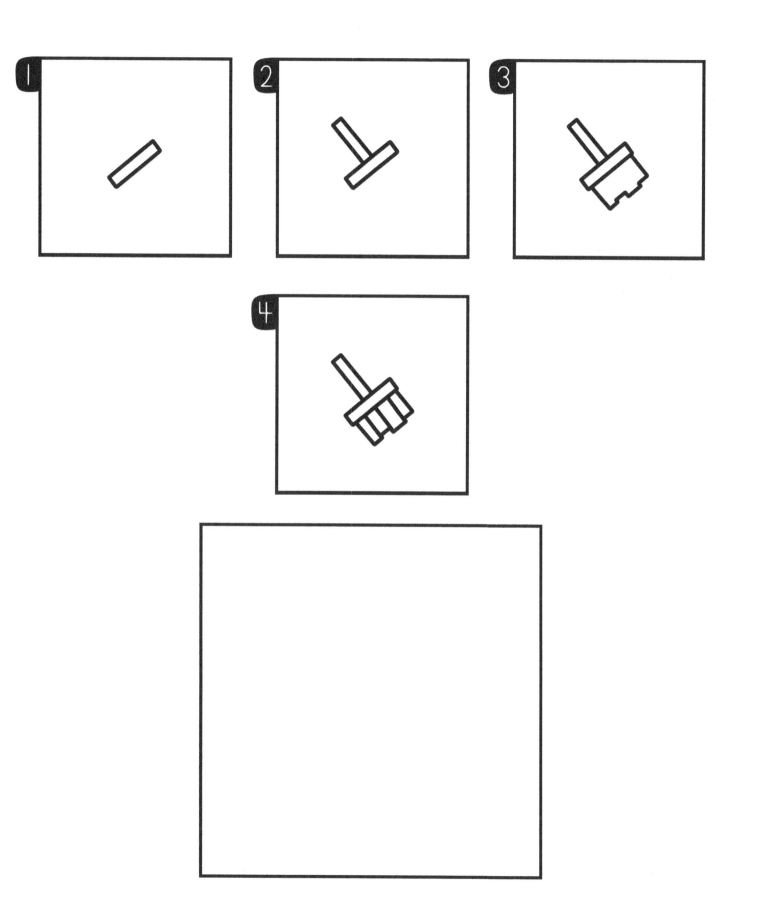

Extra Drawing Space!

Trace the Fossil Brush and color the picture.

Trace the Hexagon

A hexagon is a shape with 6 sides and 6 corners!

What part of the Stop Sign is a hexagon?

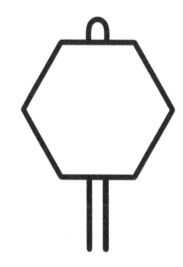

Good answer! Now turn the page to doodle a Stop Sign!

Extra Drawing Space!

Stop Sign

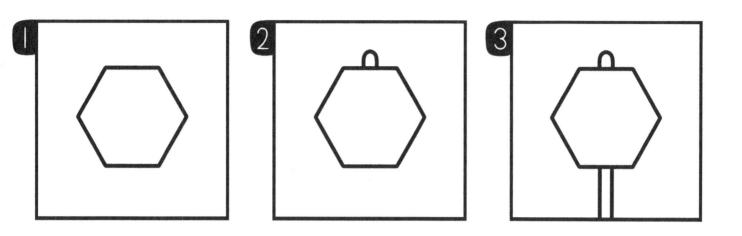

Extra Drawing Space!

Trace the Stop Sign and color the picture.

Trace the Hexagon

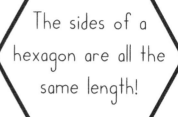

The sides of a hexagon are all the same length!

Trace the Triceratops head with your finger and count the sides!

Good job! Now turn the page to doodle a Triceratops!

Extra Drawing Space!

Triceratops

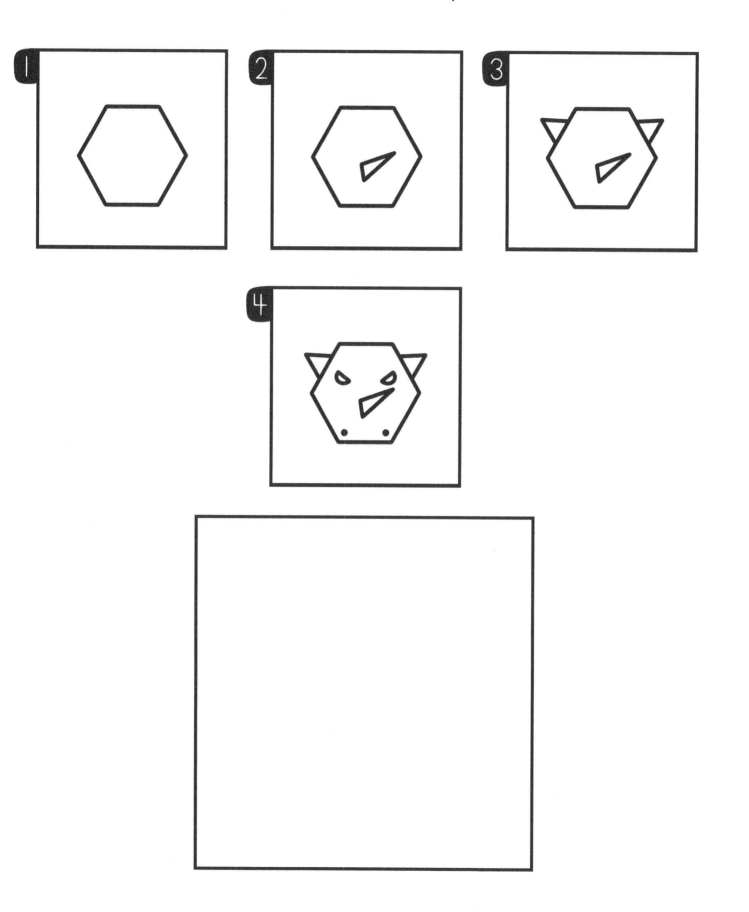

Extra Drawing Space!

Trace the Triceratops and color the picture.

Trace the Star

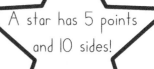

A star has 5 points and 10 sides!

Count the points of the star in the Meteor doodle!

Good job!
Now turn the page to doodle a Meteor!

Extra Drawing Space!

Meteor

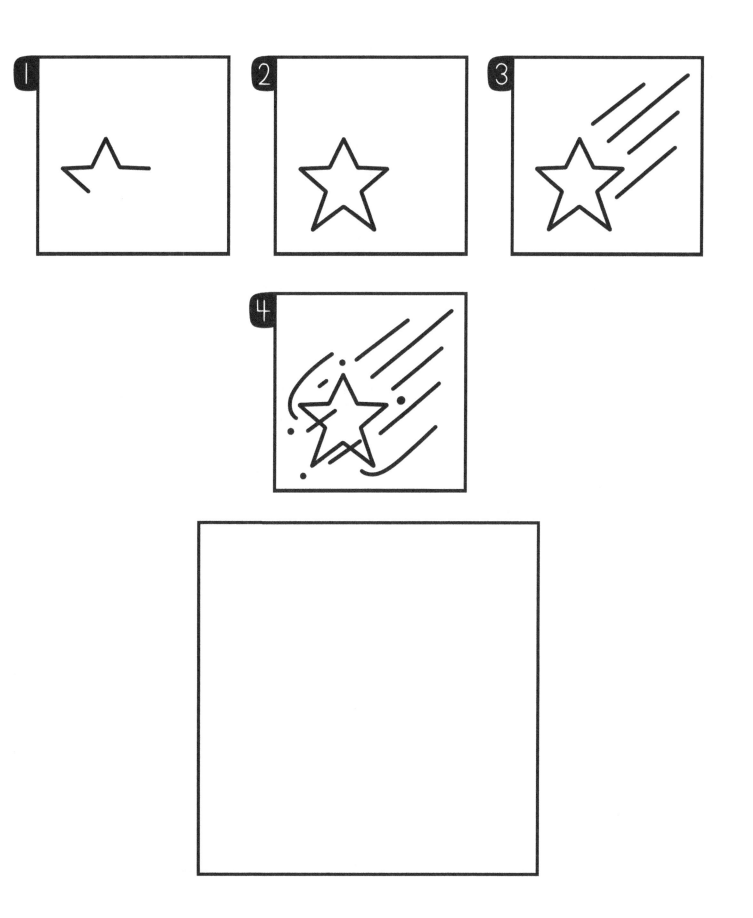

Extra Drawing Space!

Trace the Meteor and color the picture.

○ Orange   ☐ Yellow   ⬭ Red   ☆ Green   ▭ Brown   △ Light Pink   ⬡ Yellow   ⬯ Gray

○ Brown ☐ Yellow ⌒ Red ☆ Green ▭ Purple △ Pink ⬡ Light Blue ◯ Gray

○ Light Blue ☐ Purple ◠ Red ☆ Green ▭ Brown △ Pink ⬡ Gray ◯ Yellow

Find and color the shapes!

GOAL!

Find and color the shapes!

Triceratops

Stegosaurus

Sauropods

Alamosaurus

Apatosaurus

Brontosaurus

Brachiosaurus

Diplodocus

Supersaurus

More Dinos

Microraptor

Pterodactyl

Tyrannosaurus

Mixosaurus

Dilophosaurus

Spinosaurus

Extra Drawing Space!

Extra Drawing Space!

Extra Drawing Space!

Make Your Own Doodle

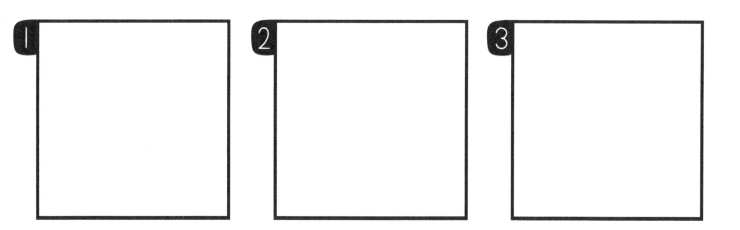

Make Your Own Doodle

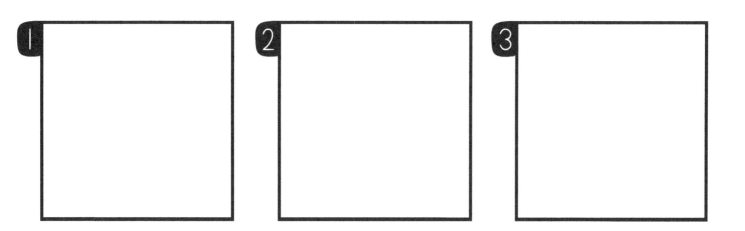

Make Your Own Doodle

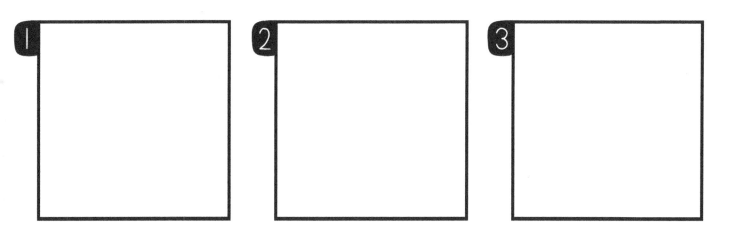

Make Your Own Doodle

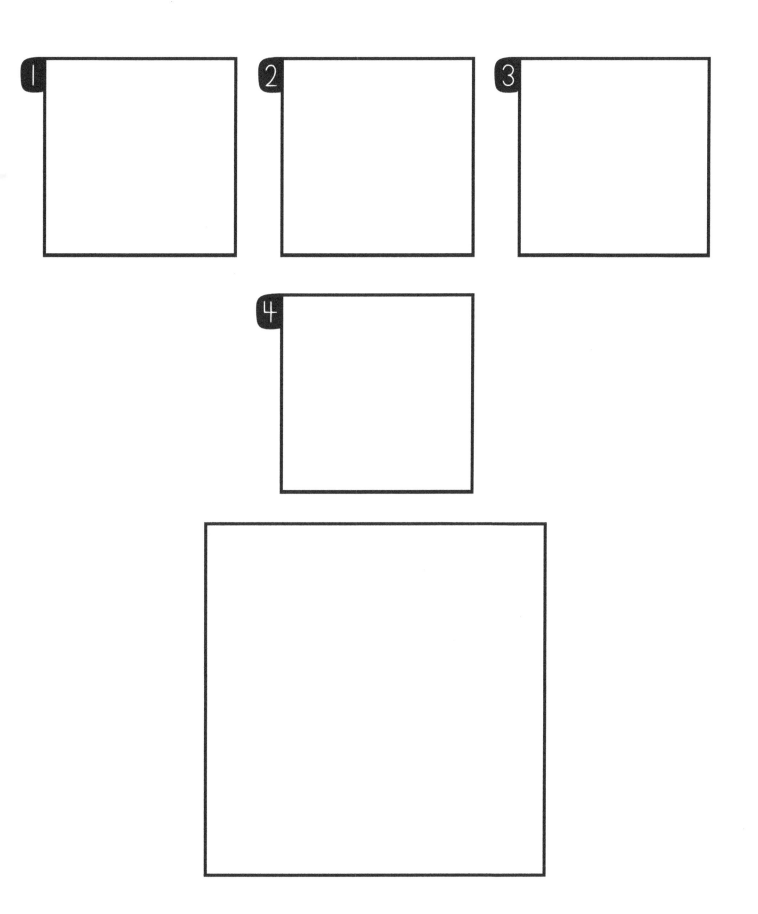

Make Your Own Doodle

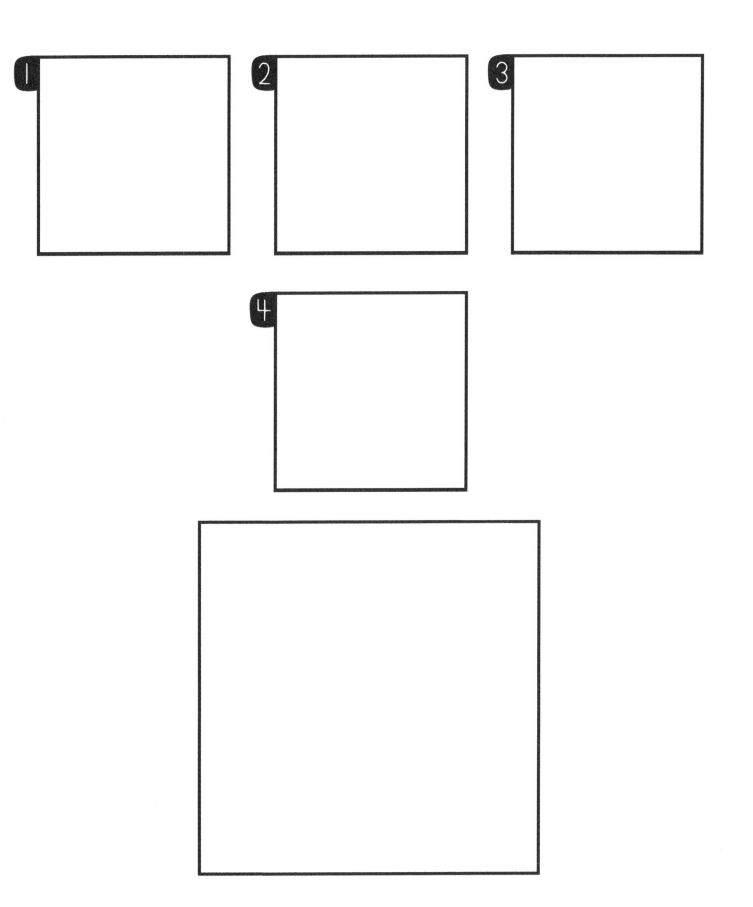

Make Your Own Doodle

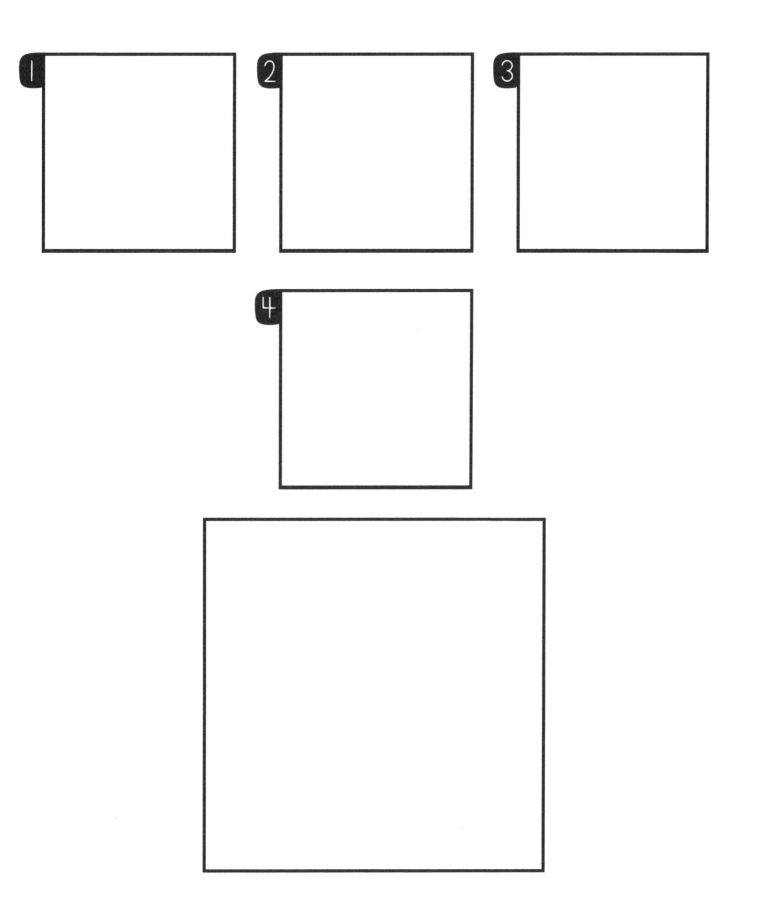

Hidden Shape Answers

Find and color the shapes!

Hidden Shape Answers

GOAL!

#1

10

Find and color the shapes!

In the Doodles Help Handwriting Series

Doodles Help Handwriting: Uppercase Letters

Doodles Help Handwriting: Lowercase Letters

Doodles Help Handwriting: More Uppercase Letters

Doodles Help Handwriting: More Lowercase Letters

Doodles Help Handwriting: Numbers

Doodles Help PRE Handwriting

Doodles Help PRE Handwriting and Counting

Doodles Help Handwriting: Baby Animal Edition

Doodles Help Handwriting: Line Work

Doodles Help Handwriting: Spacing

Adults Can Doodle Too

Made in the USA
Monee, IL
11 November 2024

69871672R00077